HOW TO BE
THE PERFECT
BEST MAN

FROM YOU & YOUR WEDDING MAGAZINE

Cathy Howes

First published in Great Britain in 2003 by
Michael O'Mara Books Limited
9 Lion Yard
Tremadoc Road
London SW4 7NQ

www.youandyourwedding.co.uk

A CIP catalogue record for this book is available from the British Library.

ISBN 1-84317-002-7

1 3 5 7 9 10 8 6 4 2

Cover photograph: Stockbyte

Designed and typeset by Design 23

www.mombooks.com

Printed and bound in Great Britain by Cox & Wyman, Reading, Berks.

CONTENTS

INTRODUCTION

Congratulations! You've just been asked to act as best man at your best mate's wedding. Naturally, you're pleased and flattered but, secretly, even thinking about the prospect terrifies you. Don't worry! We know exactly how you feel. Just relax – you're not on your own.

How To Be The Perfect Best Man will be your trusty guide every step of the way. Specially devised with the expertise of *You & Your Wedding* magazine, this practical, down-to-earth, information-packed handbook takes you through each stage of the process, and deals with all the problems that you are likely to encounter.

Packed with sound advice and brilliant hints and tips, this great little book does all the thinking for you. It makes the job of best man as effortless as possible, telling you what you have to do and when you have to do it. And, yes, this does include lots of great ideas on how to deliver your speech with style and wit. In fact, you'll find everything you need right here at your fingertips. So, forget your nerves, follow these friendly guidelines, then turn up on the day and have a great time!

You & Your Wedding is Britain's best-selling wedding magazine and is available from all good newsagents.

CATHY HOWES

THOROUGHLY MODERN...
TRADITIONALISTS

*'English law prohibits a man from marrying his
mother-in-law. This is our idea of useless legislation!'*
ANON

'We didn't do it like that in my day...' is a telling
phrase that defines the generation gap, and never
more so than during the run-up to a wedding. The
happy couple is likely to hear it quite a lot during the
months of preparation; and, as best man, so will you.
By all means listen politely to tales of yesteryear, but
be careful not to judge a 21st century wedding by
1950s standards. With a steady increase in second
marriages, the total number of weddings in 2002 rose
for the first time in a decade. Nearly a quarter of all
weddings involve one or more partner who has been
divorced or widowed; and in one in five cases both
participants are remarrying. All this can make the
problems of seating plans and what to say in speeches
complicated enough to challenge the most seasoned
diplomat.

The sky's the limit!

Despite being one of the most traditional celebrations, the modern wedding has evolved beyond recognition over the past few years. More than half of all ceremonies are now civil, largely due to the wide range of newly licensed venues. This opens up a whole new world of possibilities for originality, experimentation and themed weddings in places as diverse as a moored submarine and the London Eye. You certainly couldn't get married at London Zoo in granny's day, but you can now!

It is not only changes in the law that have updated the act of marriage. The average age of a bride and groom is now twenty-eight and thirty respectively, probably making them considerably older than their parents or grandparents were when they tied the knot. Marrying later also means that the couple is likely to be more financially secure; with the average wedding (if there is such a thing) now coming in at about £14,500, it is increasingly common for couples to foot some or all of the bill themselves. The days when the father-of-the-bride picked up the entire tab have more or less gone.

This shift of emphasis away from parental influence and back onto the couple themselves can have a significant impact on the role of the best man.

It's not just a matter of turning up on the day with polished shoes and trying to stay sober until after the speeches – your groom may be very hands-on during the preparations and may want you to immerse yourself in choosing a marquee or deciding where to display the *croquembouche*. (And if you don't know what a *croquembouche* is, you really should get a bit more wedding-savvy!)

Many of the traditions that have been followed year in, year out are beginning to change. Couples can now opt to write their own vows at civil ceremonies, some brides decide against being 'given away' and nowadays hardly anyone serves sherry at the wedding breakfast. When Brad Pitt married Jennifer Aniston, 200 guests heard him promise to 'split the difference on the thermostat' and she, in turn, vowed to keep the supply of his favourite banana milkshake coming. Things have certainly moved on from the old 'love, honour and obey' ethos. Couples are choosing a more relaxed, reportage style of photography rather than the set-piece family line-ups; and they tend to stay until the end of their reception, rather than changing into 'going away' clothes and skipping off on honeymoon almost as soon as the cake is cut.

Today's best man

One tradition that is consistently followed, however, is the appointment of a best man. Of course, the modern best man may actually be a 'she', or he may be a young seven-year-old carrying the rings on a cushion rather than in his pocket. For the sake of argument, let's assume that most best men are actually guys and old enough to sink a pint on the stag night. Even though this excludes best 'men' of the gentler or younger persuasion, much of the same advice still applies.

Great expectations

Some things don't change. Whatever the style of wedding, as best man you will still be expected to arrive with the groom and boost his confidence during the ceremony. If there aren't enough seats, the bridal car breaks down or the vicar mixes up the dates, everyone will still look to the best man to sort out the problem. And, whether the guests eat pork pies or Pacific-rim fusion cuisine, they are going to expect the best man to make a speech. So, in many ways, the best man is what he has always been – a lads' lad, a wit, a cool head and a thoroughly organized trouble-shooter who can charm all the aunties. When you look in the mirror in a few months' time to adjust your cravat or pin on your buttonhole, this is the person who should be looking straight back at you. Your mission, should you choose to accept it, starts here...

ARE YOU UP TO IT?

*'All you need in life is ignorance and confidence
then success is sure.'*
MARK TWAIN

So, at last! You've been asked to be a best man. About time too! Someone has finally seen fit to recognize your charismatic personality, organizational skills and the fact that you cut rather a dashing figure in a morning suit. If your initial reaction is to feel flattered, hold on to that feeling, because the two sentiments that usually follow are uncertainty and panic. What exactly will you have to do at this wedding and, more importantly, will you be able to do it? Surely being best man is simply a case of organizing a stag party, keeping the rings safe, making a witty speech and dancing with the bridesmaids? If only...

Think about it

Before you get too carried away, give the groom's request careful consideration. Whether the wedding is eighteen, twelve, six or three months away, will you really be able to devote the time and energy needed to – metaphorically – hold your groom's hand? The first rule of being a best man is to remember that the bride and groom are in charge (which means the bride, of course). Nevertheless, you may still be asked to offer opinions on everything from churches, castles, hotels and marquees to top hats, cars and honeymoons. This could involve a fair bit of driving up and down the motorway, and hours of patiently flicking through brochures and portfolios or surfing the internet. Moreover, you'll be expected to do all these things with the required level of enthusiasm, not with one eye on your watch or with your thoughts on that urgent meeting at work the next day.

Keep your diary free

The best man is often chosen in the early stages of the wedding preparations, and, after the initial decisions such as the date and place have been made, things can go quiet for a few months, especially if the wedding is a year or more away. But as the time draws near, your duties will start to snowball. Put a pencil line through the weekends leading up to the wedding and try not to book holidays or trips too close to the date. Your services will be required in advance – as best man and general organizer-in-chief you will be expected to attend all rehearsals and run-throughs, as well as pre-wedding parties or dinners. The groom may also be having a couple of separate 'mini' stag nights with different groups of people, say from his office or football club. In this case, he may need you to come along to help break the ice between mates who don't know each other.

Covering all the bases

Effectively, the best man is responsible for most things but in charge of very little. In other words, the couple make the decisions and it is your job to make their choices run smoothly. You won't be expected to throw up a temporary rope bridge or build a raft from old oil drums but in many other ways, this is the equivalent of a military operation. That means getting yourself organized, so write details of any dates, times, costs and contacts that affect you in a notebook or on a checklist pinned to the wall. Never scribble bits of information on dozens of Post-it notes or on the back of a cigarette packet. Better still, start a file on your computer or laptop with every piece of information you collect.

What do you need to know?

- How many guests?
- Who is supplying the buttonholes and where will they be delivered?
- Are there orders of service and who will be taking delivery of them?
- How much will the church/venue fee be, and will it have to be paid on the day? (Traditionally, financial details such as these are handled by the best man, so that the groom's attention is not distracted by money worries.)
- What time will the meal be served? And what time are you planning to make your speech?
- Who is the main contact among the catering/serving staff and will there be a master of ceremonies?
- What time will the free bar run out, and what time will the bar close?
- How easy is it to get a taxi from the reception venue after midnight? What is the number of the local taxi service?

Prepare for the worst

All this preparation might seem over the top, but if you don't have this sort of information at your fingertips, sod's law says you'll need it. The best approach is to regard the job as a challenge. For instance, traditionally it is the best man's responsibility to get the guests from the ceremony to the reception. This is no big deal if the location is only a short walk away from the church or venue and the guest list small; but if 300 friends and family are arriving from all over the world and are staying in seven different hotels, it's a nightmare! Imagine the worst-case scenario and have it covered. Hoping for the best is not an option.

It's been emotional

Many men prefer not to talk about relationships and feelings with their mates, but, while much of the fuss before a wedding centres on the bride, the groom may begin to experience isolation, anxiety and insecurity – not that he's likely to show it to you, of course. As his close friend, it's up to you to look out for the signs and be ready with a bit of confidence-boosting banter. The groom may also start panicking about the spiralling costs, so the task of helping him rationalize certain decisions (or finding more economic alternatives) may also fall to you. Whatever his concern, a really good best man needs to listen like a therapist and answer like a diplomat. If the groom wants to rant and rave about something his mother-in-law has said or done, let him blow off steam, but try not to agree with him or feed his anger. It only takes a couple of ill-chosen remarks made off-guard to land you right in the middle of family wrangles.

But the bride's never liked me!

This is not an unknown scenario. One of the few things the groom has absolute jurisdiction over is his choice of best man. In a perfect world, he would be aware of the bride's opinion and avoid choosing someone she can't stand. But this isn't an ideal world – it's a wedding with all its attendant emotions and pressures.

If you really do have a problem getting on with the bride (or *vice versa*) you may have to find a diplomatic way of saying 'no'. If you don't see eye-to-eye with her now, the chances of a reconciliation during the coming stressful months are small. Both you and the bride are likely to be tense and uncomfortable on the day, and the groom is likely to sense your negativity on the occasion, however oblivious he may be to the ill-feeling at the start. If you decide to decline on these grounds, don't be too blunt about your reasons. 'I can't stand the woman', or 'We've never got on from day one' are not constructive excuses. You and the groom share a deep friendship that neither of you wants to spoil, but he is also planning a future with the woman he loves. Don't make him choose between the two of you.

Still want to do it?

- Don't feel nervous, feel proud. Of all the blokes he could have chosen, the groom asked you. You're a central player in this production so take some pride in making it a success. If you really don't want to do it, speak up now.
- Don't go along with the role reluctantly, then, three weeks before the wedding, drop the bombshell that you can't face the prospect.
- Being best man is not just about preparing a speech and organizing a wild stag night. That's the high-profile stuff that people judge you on afterwards. A best man also quietly smooths out all the little wrinkles in the background without making a fuss.
- Grin and bear it. Within reason you'll probably have to wear what the couple ask you to, even if gold frock coats in the style of Oscar Wilde have

never really been your thing. You're playing a part in their big day, not the other way around.

♦ Once you hit 'wedding week' your life may not be your own. Come to terms with that and accept all requests for lifts, collections, deliveries and non-stop support with good grace.

Don't panic

So, are you now worried that being a best man is a nightmare of a job that will leave you emotionally drained and physically exhausted? Well, don't be! It's simply a case of knowing what might happen, just in case.

'I've always thought being a best man sounds harder than it is,' says journalist Adam Scott, who has been both best man and groom. 'Everybody talks about it non-stop in the run-up to the wedding, "the best man does this and the best man does that...", but in my experience, the best man doesn't do as much as he's led to believe. You tend to worry because it seems like you're responsible for the entire wedding, which you're not. The best man's role is all about creating the impression of being supportive. My advice – don't panic.'

It may be obvious, but...

Kerry Johnson runs wedding consultancy Happily Hitched, which offers advice on more than just how a bride should plan her table centres. From her long experience she knows where the best-laid plans fall down. Her survival tactics include the following:

- If the stag party is taking place abroad, make sure you remember your own and the groom's passports.
- Always make sure the cars have petrol in them. One best man I know found himself stranded with the groom on the M1. Both were left waiting on the hard shoulder until the groom's father arrived with emergency supplies to get them moving again. Understandably, the bride wasn't happy.
- A cliché, I know, but all too often the best man forgets the rings. Always have a back-up. Nominate somebody to call you an hour before the wedding to make sure you have them. Ask someone you trust and get them to stick to it – this is your most important job.
- Make yourself familiar with the service so you know when your big moment will arrive – many a best man has been caught day-dreaming.
- Plan your speech well in advance and try to come up with something that fits the couple. For the

wedding of a salesman, one best man I came across did a PowerPoint presentation illustrating some of the more interesting periods of the groom's life. Always find an audience of two or three friends of the bride and groom beforehand to give you an idea of how well your speech will go down. If it's the third time the bride has been married, it may be best not to mention it.

Are you up to it?

As best man you may be expected to do some or all of the following:

◆ Offer emotional support.
◆ Show an interest in the wedding preparations.
◆ Help choose the outfits for the groom's party.
◆ Help the groom choose the drinks, by going on a wine tasting or driving over to the Continent.
◆ Organize matching formal wear hire for the groom's party.
◆ Devise and book a stag party or weekend.
◆ Arrange transport for you and the groom to the church.
◆ Settle up any church/choir/crèche fees on the day.
◆ Arrange your own transport to the reception.
◆ Check that no guests have been stranded.
◆ Act as master of ceremonies or toastmaster.

- Keep an eye on the bar stocks/money behind the bar.
- Ensure wedding presents are safe.
- Make a sparkling speech.
- Offer yourself out as dance partner to unaccompanied female guests.
- Check that the couple have everything they need when they leave the reception.
- Decorate the bridal car (tastefully).
- Check nothing is left behind at the reception.
- Return the groom's hire suit.

I DON'T THINK I'M THE TYPE...

'My one regret in life is that I'm not someone else.'
WOODY ALLEN

There's no such thing as an identikit of the perfect best man any more than there is a typical groom. In fact, these days, the best man doesn't even have to be a man! Given that the duties are so varied and the responsibilities sometimes quite arduous, if a groom were able to advertise for his ideal *aide-de-camp* in the Situations Vacant column, would you recognize yourself from this?

WANTED

Competent and reliable second-in-command for short-term but high-pressure project.
Are you punctual, unflappable, charming, funny and diplomatic? Do you have sharp organizational skills, transportation knowledge, patience and understanding?
Previous public speaking experience not necessary but applicant should be willing to learn.
Ballroom dancing and photography skills a bonus.
Clean driving licence (and car) essential.

Even the most famous figures from the silver screen have had trouble filling that brief. Hugh Grant's best man in *Four Weddings And A Funeral* might have been charming and funny, but his character was about as diplomatic as *Coronation Street's* Les Battersby and as responsible as Mr Bean.

Mr Cool

The bride's car has broken down on the hard shoulder of the M25, the ovens in the kitchens of your reception venue have short-circuited and the youngest bridesmaid has just thrown up in the font. Suddenly, eighty pairs of eyes turn to look at you. Isn't the best man supposed to do something?

That means you! Of course, none of the above is likely to happen – and certainly not all at once – but a cool head often wins high praise from the mother-of-the-bride.

If a problem does crop up, take a deep breath and be realistic. There is no point in panicking about things you can't influence. Smile a lot, reassure people, get on the phone and look as if you're sorting things out, even if you are dying inside. As long as guests think that the emergency is contained they'll soon be distracted by something else. You never know what might happen at weddings – at his marriage to Bianca Jagger in Nice, Mick Jagger was famously locked out of St Anne's Chapel. The doors were barred to keep out the fans, but they managed to lock out the groom too! So, your job is to keep an eye out for any signs that plans are going awry. Relax, it'll be fine. Your groom is not a Rolling Stone.

Mr Responsible

Don't stuff the inside top pocket of your suit with mints or small accessories that you think you might need if you get lucky at the reception. This is where you safely tuck away the precious rings (in some cases these are worth thousands of pounds) and this is where they should still be when you're asked to produce them during the ceremony. Richard Gere and Cindy Crawford may have been happy enough to swap hastily concocted rings made from aluminium foil for their wedding at the Little Church of the West in Las Vegas, but your happy couple will want to celebrate their union with their own carefully chosen wedding bands. So guard them with your life.

Accidents can happen!

When Peter Jenkins acted as best man for his brother Tony, some years ago in Glasgow, the brothers followed the old tradition of throwing 'bill money' to the local children as the car set off for the church. Basically, the car pulls away quite slowly, then as the vehicle gathers pace, the local children run behind as the groom and best man throw out small coins to the youngsters. This Scottish tradition is known as a 'scramble', although Peter was later to call it a disaster. As a collection of 5p and 10p pieces flew out of the window, so did the bride's ring. The brothers only discovered their plight when they arrived at the church and had to hurriedly retrace their steps. Fortunately, one honest little soul had picked it up and handed it in, but it was a close call.

In addition to guarding the rings, the best man often has to look after other crucial items. For instance, you may have to carry important documentation such as divorce papers, or cash given to you by the groom to pay for the priest, choir, registrar, hotel bar, DJ, etc. If you're the type who puts his briefcase on the roof of the car while unlocking the door, then forgets it's there and drives away, think seriously about whether you are ideally suited to take on all this responsibility. In the real world, people usually forgive well-meaning scatterbrains for their little oversights – at weddings they are inclined to lynch them.

Mr Diplomatic

You'll have to start thinking like a politician. Imagine a few typical scenarios: the groom likes the stately home; the bride won't get married unless it's at the castle. His mother thinks a buffet would be best; her mother will not budge an inch on the sit-down meal. Be careful to stay neutral. If someone asks you whether you think the pageboys look sweet in tangerine, avoid the temptation to remark that they actually look like they've been Tangoed.

But be careful not to let your 'I'm-soooo-interested-in-everything-about-this-wedding' expression land you in trouble. The next question could be, 'Let's ask the best man what he thinks…' and you could find yourself faced with a problem that has no answer. If you are caught in the middle of the cross-fire, bow out gracefully and practise a few of these get-out-of-jail-free phrases:

- 'God, is that the time? I must pick up my gran from the dentist.'
- 'Whose car alarm is that? Don't worry, I'll go.'
- 'Can anyone else smell burning?'
- 'It's so hot in here, I think I'm going to faint.'

Mr Modest

During the big day you may be faced with a dilemma that takes all your reserves of ingenuity and quick thinking. In a tricky situation, even though you're not responsible for the mess-up, you are likely to be responsible for the solution. Once you've sorted it out, however, do resist the temptation to tell everyone what an amazing bloke you are. Solve the problem and move swiftly on. Don't spend forty minutes telling the happy couple – who have better things to do – how you saved the day. Ideally, they will never know just how brilliant a best man you were until some time after the event.

Mr Charming

You may be wearing the Fred Astaire suit, but have you got the footwork? If the structure of the reception includes an official first dance, once the happy couple have taken a few steps around the dance floor, it could be your turn next. You may be dreaming of that scene from *My Best Friend's Wedding:* 'It is the duty of the best man to dance with the matron of honour and I've got moves that you haven't seen before!' was a tempting invitation indeed from Julia Roberts to teenage best man Scotty. But that's Hollywood, not real life.

Fancy footwork

Traditionally, after the bride, groom and their parents have danced to a few bars of music, the best man asks the chief bridesmaid or matron of honour to dance. This is one of the details that you should confirm beforehand. Have the couple chosen a first dance and do they want to follow that particular route? If they do, try not to be in the gents, making a call on your mobile or outside having a quick cigarette when the time comes. And don't panic if you're not the world's greatest dancer – a little rhythmic swaying is usually enough.

'You dancin'?'

During the evening's dancing keep an eye out for women who don't have partners. While no one expects you to turn into a gigolo, it is always a thoughtful gesture to ask a single lady or widowed auntie to dance. Don't press your case, though. If they say no, they probably mean it. You are the best man, after all, not a Butlin's Red Coat.

Mr Prepared

Although you may not have been closely involved with the catering arrangements, if it suddenly turns out that there are not enough soft drinks for the children, or there are more vegetarians than was first thought, the guests or venue staff will invariably consult the best man first. Try to sort out hassles like these without troubling the couple or the top table. This is why best men were invented. If it means putting your hand in your pocket for a little bit extra, only you know whether or not the groom would be happy to extend the budget by that amount. If he hasn't given you a cash float for the day, pay the extra out of your own money and keep a receipt. Don't spoil the flow of the day by mentioning it to him now, and never ask for the money back straightaway!

When French screen idol Gerard Depardieu married his wife Elisabeth, he chose old friend Michel Pilorge to be his best man. When Pilorge met the groom's parents from the railway station, Depardieu's father Dédé not only wore a suit that looked thirty years old with frayed shirt cuffs dangling from his sleeves, but once they arrived at the reception, Dédé was not impressed with the champagne and liqueurs on offer. 'He was in desperate need of a glass of red wine,' Pilorge told Depardieu's biographer Paul Chutkow, so the best man accompanied the father-of-the-groom outside and found him a café where he could sit and knock back a few glasses of reassuring *vin rouge*.

Ready for anything

Bob Wheeler was best man to Julian Perring. 'I was absolutely terrified before the speeches,' he says. 'My throat was drying up and I was shaking like a leaf. I think I was in a completely different zone from anyone else. I'd prepared till I was blue in the face. It's not my nature to leave things to chance. I wouldn't say I spent weeks on it but every time a thought came into my head I wrote it down and then put them all in order as the day drew nearer. I decided to learn my speech off by heart – and I did, although I had it written out in front of me as a prompt. I didn't need the notes in the end because I knew it back to front. Because I'd rewritten it so many times it still seemed quite fresh.

'Once I started it went down really well. The bride's parents had both died the previous year and in his speech Julian obviously made a mention about them not being there which brought a few tears to a few eyes. It was touching and I think everyone appreciated it. It was my job to follow up with the next speech and lift the spirits again. I even invited a little heckling to avoid it just being my voice. I wanted to hear laughter and some appreciation of the comments I was making. One thing I realized very early on was that everyone there was on my side.

They were friends and people close to me, so there was no way I was going to go wrong. I enjoyed being best man and it was a really fulfilling role. It was lovely to be part of something that was so memorable. My advice would be to plan everything, not just the speech, as well as you can. Think about things. Don't just assume everything will go right on the day. Work out all the details and have some options or a way out of any possible problems.'

Have you got what it takes?

- A cool head. Your job is to keep the groom calm and collected.
- A safe pair of hands. Those rings are worth a lot of money!
- The tact of a diplomat. Weddings are very emotional and when the booze is flowing, tears often follow.
- A modest nature. The idea is to work quietly and efficiently in the background, not to take centre stage.
- A large serving of charm. A little flattery can go a long way.
- The training of a boy scout. Be prepared for anything.

THE BIG BUILD-UP

*'If people turn to look at you on the street,
you are not well-dressed.'*
BEAU BRUMMELL

Although the best man may get involved with many aspects of the wedding planning along the way, his opinion is often only sought after the couple have more or less made up their minds on something and just need reassurance. Basically, they want you to agree with them. If you are wearing your diplomat's hat, you will tell them what they want to hear. But you also have to be Mr Practical. If the couple get over-ambitious and start to introduce unnecessary or complicated layers into the proceedings, it is also your place to gently point out the pitfalls. Apart from anything else, if everything starts to unravel horribly on the day, *you* will be in charge of damage limitation!

One of the areas you will probably become involved with personally is the style of the groom's clothes, which will also dictate your own outfit on the day. Again, the bride is likely to want to have a say in this – some brides more than others – but the choice should ultimately be the groom's as he's the guy who has to wear it.

Spoilt for choice

Most couples marrying at a register office tend to steer away from full morning wear with top hats. There is no real reason for this other than the fact that tails seem too formal for a shorter, low-key ceremony and there is usually limited space. Although black tie is traditionally not worn until after 6pm, couples are increasingly throwing these social restrictions out of the window. Black tie has always been very popular at Jewish weddings, and it is now worn frequently at register offices, as it is dressy without being too formal.

For civil ceremonies held at the increasingly wide choice of stately homes, hotels and other licensed venues, as with religious weddings, the choice is between formal wear, occasion wear and the traditional smart lounge suit. Just as women go shopping together for their wedding outfits, so the best man plays a key role in helping the groom choose the men's dress code.

Morning glory

A morning suit can come in a variety of styles and colours. Traditionally, it is composed of a black, grey or navy single-breasted tail coat, pinstripe trousers, a tunic or wing-collar shirt with a silk tie. Some grooms choose a cravat, which is an American accessory, in place of a tie. The outfit is completed with a top hat which is carried rather than worn. Waistcoats can be plain to match the suit or in a colour theme to pick up the bride's flowers or the bridesmaids' dresses.

When you try on a morning suit, check for ripples in the cloth the way you would for a lounge suit. If the sleeves come up short, try another jacket. The sleeves should fall just past your watch but not cover the bottom of your hand. Check for tightness across the shoulders, chest or stomach and make sure the tail section is well cut and hangs neatly with the correct amount of curve or tailoring at the small of the back. If you are hiring, be aware that big occasions such as Royal Ascot, Henley Royal Regatta, Cartier International Polo at Windsor, Glorious Goodwood and Glyndebourne may all have a knock-on effect on availability in high season.

Morning wear checklist

Ede & Ravenscroft have been making coronation robes for more than 300 years, so they know a thing or two about dressing for occasions. Their top tips are:

- If hiring a morning suit, wear braces. Hired trousers may not be the perfect fit.
- If you are wearing a stiff collar with morning wear, take a spare one each for emergencies.
- Avoid wearing shirts straight out of the packet. Shirts should be laundered once before you wear them to lose any stiffness.
- Make sure the flower goes through the buttonhole on the lapel. Don't make the mistake of pinning it to the lapel. A good suit will have silk thread behind the button hole to hold the stem in place.
- Wear a good quality silk tie rather than a cravat, together with a double-cuffed shirt with cufflinks.
- Have a full dress rehearsal with your groom at least two weeks before the wedding to iron out any problems.

Frock tactics

Some men initially dismiss the idea of a colourful or silk frock coat or Nehru jacket as being a bit flamboyant, but king of cool David Beckham went for this style, and no one doubts his iconic status in the fashion world. This is one of those design decisions that must be down to the groom. He may want his whole male party to wear the same style, or he may want to stand out with a velvet number and ask his ushers and best man to wear more muted versions.

Whatever your groom chooses – black tie, tails, Edwardian frock coat or the Mr Darcy look – the chances are that some or all of the party will have to hire the clothes. The prospect may seem daunting, but the perfect best man should have it covered! We put the most frequently asked questions about hiring formal wear to Steve Hubbard, controller for formal hire at the Burton group, which has 175 branches around the country.

When to order?

'For us the wedding year starts from September through to the following August,' Steve says. 'The enquiry stage is usually September through to Christmas/January. This is when grooms and their best men are doing their research and looking at brochures. Don't be embarrassed at this stage to ask about etiquette. No one will expect you to know when to wear a wing collar. Usually the groom will have asked a few questions at store level and may revisit from the middle of January through to April/May when the majority of bookings come through. Bookings through the summer tend to be a bit more drip-fed as the weddings take place. If there are other things happening, whether it's Royal Ascot in June, peak time for weddings in July/August, or even if you want a highland outfit around Hogmanay, don't leave it too late to book.

'Even though we have six million units of stock, if you want something a little unusual or if you are not a standard size, there might be a limited quantity. Grooms can arrange their clothes as much as a year ahead but on average a good three months is normal. Obviously it depends on how fussy the groom is and how far in advance the bride has organized her clothes and her bridesmaids' colour scheme. It's best to leave enough time to have a good hunt round for an appropriate waistcoat or neckwear to co-ordinate with bride, flowers or bridesmaid. Three months leaves enough time for ushers or male family members in different parts of the country to call into their local branch.'

What's the best way to co-ordinate this?

'To make sure members of the groom's party all get the same outfit even though they are at opposite ends of the country, grooms can use a multi-site order form which is co-ordinated from the groom's branch. He makes his selection then gives the details to the other members of his wedding party to take into their local branch to register the selection. If he risks doing it by phone, different guests could end up with a different shade of navy or a tail coat instead of a frock coat. Hopefully, this eliminates the margin for error, although with the best will in the world there is always the chance of human error or a system error. When people are geographically apart, they are all in blissful ignorance that something has gone wrong until they all get side by side together at the wedding. This is where the best man comes in. He can act as a co-ordinator/organizer just by calling round all members of the hire party and talking them through their outfits, checking "Have you got X or Y?" etc.'

What sort of sizing problems might there be?

'Selected ranges go up to a 60-inch chest, for the rather big gentleman. The danger is if people assume that their size will be available and don't do their homework. Body builders, for example, might have problems because a jacket will be fine in the chest, but far too big and baggy around the waist. If you consider you've got a 6- to 8-inch drop between your chest and waist measurement, it may well not fit properly. The outfits are all made to a similar block and therefore if you are non-standard, you should consider a made-to-measure suit. We made suits for the England football squad and there were players with such solid thighs that they had to have a trouser waist four inches bigger than the actual waist to get the right thigh measurement and then tie them in with a belt.'

When are the clothes collected and returned?

'We try to get outfits in store seven to ten days before the event for the fitting to check everything in the outfit is exactly what was required. Now is the time to check that the suit is not too tight, too small or too short in the leg. Maybe the father-of-the-bride has lost some weight from the shell shock of how much it has cost him! – it's best to be sure. When the groom and his party come in for a fitting, if everything's fine, they take their suits away there and then. If a changeover is needed, we try to get it swapped, which is why we need a few days. Outfits are usually returned on the first working day after the wedding.'

What happens if the suits are torn or stained at the reception?

'Don't attempt to sponge or clean them. In Burton's case, each suit is bar coded so it has a complete history of when it was bought, who's hired it, who's cleaned it, when it was sent out. When the groom, best man, ushers, or whoever, order a suit, they pay 50% deposit for the value of the hire and an accidental damage waiver of a few pounds in case it is ripped or stained with red wine. The only thing that isn't covered by accidental damage waiver in our case is the top hat because photographers have a habit of asking the wedding party to chuck their hats in the air for an animated photo. Half of them catch them and half of them don't and this can become very expensive!'

More details of Burton's formal hire are available at www.burtonmenswear.co.uk

Lounge lizards

Always reassure the groom – and his fiancée, if necessary – that choosing a smart lounge suit is not a cop-out and needs no apology. A sharp, well-made suit looks just as impressive in the photos as a velvet jacket or a top hat. But as best man you will have to be a bit strict here and crack the style whip, as without a formal dress code, you are leaving key male players to their own devices.

As co-ordinator of the ushers, it is up to you to make sure they all understand that they should be smart and clean; they are not to turn up in the same old work suit that has seen better days or is shiny or worn in any way. The ushers are the first people the guests see when they arrive at the ceremony, so missing buttons or frayed cuffs are completely unacceptable. Hopefully, you'll already know the sartorial savages among your ushers in time to step in and check that they understand the meaning of 'smart'.

Looking good

- ◆ Short in the leg? A pinstripe will give the impression of a couple of extra inches. Go for slim-fitting, flat-fronted trousers and avoid anything cut with a wide leg.
- ◆ Carrying extra weight? A classic double-breasted jacket will work better than a single. Avoid flat-fronted trousers and opt for a single pleat instead.
- ◆ Skin and bones? Wear a single-breasted jacket open to give the impression of extra pounds. Go for a fitted shape on the shoulder but not too fitted on the waist and choose a slightly heavier fabric – like a wool flannel – to give yourself a bit of body.

- Big in the chest? Large-chested men, particularly body builders, often have shoulders that look twice the width of their hips, giving them a triangular look. An open-buttoned frock coat works well with this physique.
- Get shirty. On no account choose a shirt with short sleeves or pockets. This is the one occasion when it pays to buy a decent shirt from an expert. French shirt-maker Alain Figaret recommends a style with hidden buttons, a large open or full cutaway collar and double cuffs. A collar made from two pieces of material sits better and also means you can use collar stiffeners. A split yoke – the vertical cut at the back of the collar – also gives the collar a better 'seat'.
- Accessories. Ties are essentially British, cravats American. Shoes should be black and polished with matching socks. Don't bother with gloves – they are a bit formal – and only carry your top hat, don't wear it.

Alex Little was best man to Kieran O'Byrne whom he's known since sixth-form college.

'I wasn't involved much in the wedding preparations although I did offer,' he says. 'The couple seemed to have everything in hand – the bride's wedding machine, as I called it, was already in full swing. I didn't have to organize the stag night, as I don't live locally to Kieran. That was done by someone who did. We went go-karting, then back to Kieran's place for a few drinks and some pizza, then London's West End to a bar and a club. There were no strippers involved – nothing sleazy at all. For the wedding, Kieran wanted the men's dress code kept simple and chose black tie, which was fine because most of us had our own dinner suits. I got mine from a charity shop a while back and have been putting it all together over the years. No one twigged on the day, although I think I probably told most people!'

Drinking and driving

Other tasks which seem to gravitate towards the groom and best man – or perhaps it's the guys who gravitate towards them? – are choosing the bridal transport and organizing the booze. Traditionally, the wedding cars are the groom's domain and the responsibility for transportation of guests falls to the best man. Often this involves little more than making sure everyone has a lift and knows where they are going. However, couples are increasingly opting to ferry their guests in groups using anything from a coach to an old London bus, in which case exact numbers are important. The transport should be booked at least six months in advance and as invitations generally only go out to guests six to eight weeks beforehand, you will not have an exact head count until quite close to the wedding.

Kerry Johnson, who runs wedding consultancy Happily Hitched, believes part of the best man's job is to make the groom feel just as special as the bride. 'It's always nice to surprise him,' she says. 'Why not arrange to hire or borrow a sports car to take you both to the wedding? Who says the bride is the only one who can have a fancy carriage?'

Choosing the booze

If the caterers at the venue are not supplying the alcohol, you could find yourself on a Channel ferry one weekend with an empty car boot and a groom with a bulging wallet. This is actually one of the more enjoyable tasks that can fall to a best man, so a little background reading wouldn't go amiss. Try Oz Clark's new *Pocket Wine Book*, £9.99 (Time Warner).

When buying alcohol for a large function such as a wedding, the rule of thumb is usually to allow between half a bottle and a full bottle per adult, although guests are going to be drinking all day and many will get through considerably more. If your groom is wavering or worrying about the expense, urge him to err on the side of extravagance. There is nothing more mortifying than running out of booze. After all, it won't go to waste, it can be used later and if he chooses his wines and champagnes wisely, they will be a tasty reminder of the big day a few weeks or months down the line. If you're buying the wines in the UK, find a wine merchant who practises a drink or return policy, so you can get your money back on any bottles that are unopened and undamaged.

Communication is the key

If it looks as though you are going to be heavily involved in the arrangements, you are going to need a system. Post-it notes and phone numbers scribbled on your hand are not going to cut it.

◆ Gather e-mail addresses of all key players, ie the ushers, the bridesmaids, the parents of both the bride and groom, and send regular round robins. These may confirm something has been booked, that the groom has chosen the style of suit he wants for the wedding party, or the fact that helping hands are needed for a trip to France to pick up the vino!

◆ Get everyone to store each other's mobile numbers

on their phones as bits of paper get lost easily. This is a good precaution should anything crop up unexpectedly on the day.

♦ If you're an internet freak, offer to set up a simple website with details of the day, travel arrangements, local hotel arrangements and a brief schedule of the day's proceedings. (For instance, guests like to know what time food is likely to be served so that they can plan lunch arrangements if necessary.) Never do anything like this without checking with the couple first, though. If they seem keen on the idea but embarrassed to ask you to go to all that trouble, offer to do it for them as their wedding present. Then that's another tick on your to-do list.

Is it covered?

♦ Does everyone in the groom's party know what he is meant to be wearing?
♦ Have the outfits been ordered in time?
♦ Are you responsible for getting guests from ceremony to reception?
♦ Will the ring boxes fit in your pocket or will you need something else to carry them in?
♦ Have you got a running order of the day's schedule?
♦ Have you run the speech past the groom yet?

- Does everyone know the date and cost of the stag party?
- How will the couple get from the reception to their hotel?
- How much cash will you need during the day to settle fees and bills?
- Have you booked yourself in for a haircut?

THE FINAL COUNTDOWN

*'If everything's under control, you're not
going fast enough.'*
MARIO ANDRETTI

There's a great episode of *Friends,* just before Ross's
wedding, when best man Joey gets off with a stripper
and wakes up the next morning to find the precious
wedding ring missing. Has he been robbed by his one-
night stand? As it happens, his pet duck swallowed it,
but the moral of the story is obvious: don't leave things
to chance (or near anything with a beak). Everything
that has been discussed and picked over in detail for
months suddenly snowballs and you have to keep up.
This is when you may begin to wish you had given
every wedding conversation your rapt attention!

Questions, questions

'Are you collecting the orders of service? No? Then
who is?' 'Where is the florist dropping off the
buttonholes – at the church or the bride's mum's
house?' 'How are they getting to the church?' 'Did
anyone tell the venue management that there are two
wheelchair users in the party? Would you be a darling
and just give them a call?' This is where the willing

49

helper and diplomat come into play. Try not to take it personally if the bride, groom or any of their close family get a bit snappy. They're just tense. (Did we mention you may have to be whipping boy, too?) You may need to turn on the charm in these final busy days, but save plenty of reserves for the female guests and the dance floor at the wedding.

One week before

- The rehearsal will probably be this week. Turn down anything else that crops up, however tempting, to ensure you are available. After all, if you don't know what's going to be happening on the day, how on earth is anyone else supposed to?

- What, no speech? Even if it's not typed to perfection, it should be in some sort of shape by now. Hoping for divine inspiration or a thunderbolt of creativity on the morning of the wedding won't work.

- Double-check that there are no major road works/rail engineering works/big sporting events that could affect guests coming from out of town, or throw out your timings from house to ceremony or ceremony to reception. It only takes one set of emergency traffic lights or a lane closed on an A road to add fifteen minutes onto a finely timed journey.

- Could your hair do with a trim?

Two days before

+ Give your shirt a gentle iron and hang it up out of harm's way.

+ Remove the prices from the bottom of any new shoes and try lightly scratching the surface of the soles with something sharp or abrasive to make them less slippery. Remind the groom to do the same with his shoes.

+ You should have collected any hired formal wear by now. Try on the whole ensemble, whether it's a morning suit, black tie or a tailored lounge suit. It's no good finding out on the morning of the wedding that you need a new belt/braces/a different tie/ another shirt.

+ 'It is absolutely imperative that someone has given you a checklist of everything scheduled throughout the day,' says wedding co-ordinator Toni Henningsohn, 'from when the cars are going to arrive, to when the entertainment finishes. If you haven't got someone controlling the time, it is very easy to start running late.'

+ Ring all your ushers to check how they are getting to the ceremony. This will give you a rough idea of cars and possible lifts to offer stranded guests. Remind them to be there early.

Putting on a show

Jason Hall is an actor and casting director who was best man to fellow actor Darren. In keeping with their profession, the bride and groom were married in an old Victorian theatre in Portsmouth. 'I'm in London so wasn't too involved with the early planning, but I had all my tasks outlined for when we got down to Portsmouth the night before,' says Jason. 'They actually got married on the stage with the congregation in what was the Circle. The reception was held in what was the Stalls.

'This was great from a best man's point of view because the guests didn't leave the building, which made the job a lot easier because I (and the ushers) only had to guide people around three or four rooms. A lot of actors were invited so it took place on a Sunday. We couldn't get into the venue the day before so had to be there very early on the Sunday. For instance, the music and disco equipment couldn't be visible during the ceremony, so the guests had drinks in the bar while we moved everything. It was like putting on a show for the first time. We'd had our running order but there was no time for a rehearsal. We just talked it all through the day before in great detail. It was my first experience as a best man and I've never been married either, so

I was surprised at the work involved. It was hard on the couple and you could really see the pressure on their faces at times!'

The day before

♦ Wedding co-ordinator Toni Henningsohn advises that someone – whether it's the bride, her mother or the best man – should ring round every supplier the day before and confirm they have the correct booking and the right date. It has been known for a supplier to say, 'Oh, I thought that was next week'. If you haven't been asked to do this, check that someone has.

♦ Some couples like to give guests who are staying in local hotels or guest houses welcome bags containing brochures, little maps and contact details for the venues and the key players (ie the couple and you). If you're responsible for these, take them to the hotel reception and ask if they can be given to the guests as they sign in or, even better, left in their rooms.

♦ Give your car a good clean and throw away any clutter. Make sure it has plenty of petrol and water. Put any ribbons on the front seat of the car so that you don't forget to tie them on in all the chaos of tomorrow's activities.

- Whether you prefer squash, weights or a run, take some exercise to release feel-good endorphins and get the circulation going. You'll need all your wits about you tomorrow. Finish with a steam bath or sauna to relax your muscles.

The night before

- Are you sure you're not supposed to be collecting or delivering anything?
- Wrap your wedding present and write out your card, if you haven't already done so.
- Have one last run through your speech in front of the mirror and put it somewhere safe.
- Smart money would suggest you have a light evening meal and an early night, but you are best man, not best boy, so use your own judgement. If it's going to be a few beers with the guys, perhaps you should leave out the yeasty real ale and a curry to finish. Enough said.

I've got your number

Make a note of all the telephone numbers you may need on the day, just in case people don't turn up as expected, or end up going to the wrong place, and keep it with your mobile phone. Better still, if there's enough room in the memory, key them into your phone. You can delete them straight after the wedding.

Local taxi firm_____

Address of the house the bride will be leaving from

_____

_____

Father-of-the-bride's mobile,
if he has one_____

Car hire firm_____

Florists_____

Reception venue_____

Cake-maker_____

Reception DJ_____

Band or entertainment_____

ON THE DAY

*'I'm a firm believer in getting married early in
the morning. That way, if it doesn't work, you haven't
wasted the whole day.'*
MICKEY ROONEY

Think of a wedding as a theatrical production. If the
bridal couple are the stars, then the best man is a
combination of producer, director, stage manager and
gaffer. You may, in turn, be needed to arrange last-
minute transport, settle nerves and bills, direct
guests, locate missing suppliers and deliver a
cracking speech. Being charming, well-groomed and
wearing a smile are essential.

BEFORE THE CEREMONY

Synchronize watches

Don't let life imitate art. The opening sequence of
Four Weddings And A Funeral – when Hugh Grant
oversleeps, is late for the church and forgets the
rings – should be a stern warning to any best man
(although it could be said that any groom who
chooses a best man with quite such an unreliable
reputation deserves all he gets). Whether the

wedding is at 11am or 4pm, plan the day like a military manoeuvre. Draw up a rough schedule for yourself and allow twenty minutes either way for luck and unforeseen circumstances. For instance, you may pencil in breakfast for 9am and it may take your groom only five minutes to eat his Weetabix, but if he disappears into the bathroom until 10am, or suddenly decides to go for a run to work off some nerves, you're on the back foot before you start.

Fill the car with petrol

A best man needs a reliable car. There may be last-minute collections or deliveries of items such as buttonholes to be covered, so get these jobs out of the way as soon as possible. You never know when some other unexpected task may crop up, such as collecting guests from the station. Cars also have a maddening tendency to break down when you least want them to, not just guests' but suppliers'. It may be the cake-maker's responsibility to deliver the cake, but if her car cuts out, someone may have to come to the rescue. The phrase, 'That's not my job' just doesn't enter the equation. Make sure you have change for parking meters, just in case, and keep a variety of cards from local mini-cab firms in your pocket.

Keep spirits up (and beer consumption down)

It is very tempting to open a bottle or visit the pub with the groom, ushers, brothers and close friends, but this is where a best man has to tread carefully between being an entertainment rep and a Sunday school teacher. Of course it's hard to tell your 15-stone, rugby-playing mate not to drink on an empty stomach or to say 'no' to a third pint, but adrenalin and nerves can play havoc with even the most hardened drinker. Imagine the groom tripping over the church steps or slurring his vows? Just don't go there! Try to delay starting on the alcohol until as late as possible. Kissing aunties and grannies with beery breath doesn't always go down well either, so stock up on extra-strong mints.

Mobile mania

As head of logistics, the best man should carry a mobile at all times – set on vibrate if you have the facility – because someone needs to be a main point of contact. If your phone doesn't have a mute option, make absolutely sure it is OFF before the ceremony and ensure all the ushers and guests do the same. This is something ushers can mention as they show guests to their seats. If there are no ushers, nominate someone else to be on mobile-silencing duty or add that to your list of tasks.

Seating arrangements

As the church or venue fills up, ushers should direct guests to their seats, to the left for the bride's family and friends and right for the groom's. This is usually covered during any rehearsal, but on the day excitement can take over. For instance, the front row on the bride's side may fill up, leaving no room for the bride's father to slip in on the end after he has escorted his daughter up the aisle. These things are unlikely, but it's as well to keep an eye out for them. If you are helping to co-ordinate the ushers, make sure you are not caught out of place with the sudden arrival of the bride. Your place is at the front on the right-hand side, to the right of the groom.

At many civil venues, seating arrangements will be slightly different, although most will still have the left-hand/right-hand divisions. If one side starts to look conspicuously emptier than the other, suggest to the ushers that they ask some guests – particularly if they are friends rather than family – whether they would mind sitting on the side with fewer people. Point out that they will be able to see better from nearer the front. It is not written anywhere that people have to sit strictly on one side, and it can look rather unbalanced to have lots of full rows opposite lots of empty ones. Once the bride's mother has taken her seat, it's usually a sign that the bride has arrived and if you're not where you should be, you need to move pronto.

Leave in plenty of time

When Red Noel was best man to Roy Madray, he wasn't responsible for getting the groom to the church, and it was probably just as well. Having had a wild time at the stag party the night before, Red and another friend were already running late for their journey from the Isle of Dogs on the north side of the Thames in London to Sidcup in Kent. 'It was a boiling hot day and we were stuck in traffic on the approach road to the Blackwall Tunnel,' he remembers. 'The car started to overheat and we just managed to make it to a petrol station before it completely broke down with steam gushing out. We called the breakdown service, but they quoted us something like two hours, which would never have got us there in time. It was so warm, loads of other drivers were having the same problem.

'We were really panicking by now as we still had quite a way to go. Suddenly, this elderly man pulled up and jokingly asked if we were going to a wedding – which we obviously were, standing there in our smart suits – and told us to jump in and he would drive us. You can't believe how relieved I was. We were still late and held everything up a bit – we arrived after the bride! – but they had to wait for us because I had the rings. We were so grateful to the guy in the car, we asked him to join us for the photos. It was quite funny really – a bridal party line-up with a complete stranger right on the end. We invited him back to the reception, too, and he even brought his wife along!'

DURING THE CEREMONY

Whether there are ushers or not, the groom and best man should arrive in plenty of time. Wedding co-ordinator Kerry Johnson believes you can't be too early. 'The men should usually aim to arrive at the venue up to an hour before the ceremony is due to start,' she says. 'This gives enough time to ensure that the minister or registrar is happy, the ushers are in place and that you are ready to greet all the guests.' Even if you don't allow yourself quite that long, get there at least half an hour beforehand. Guests may turn up early, particularly if they are from out of town and unsure of where they are going and how long it might take them to get there. Naturally, they will be relieved to see a familiar face and know that they have arrived at the right place. This also leaves you enough time to check that any last-minute deliveries of buttonholes or order of service sheets are exactly where they should be.

Ring of confidence

Check for the final time that you have the ring; in many cases you may be looking after two rings, as seventy-five per cent of men now wear a wedding band too. After that, stop checking. Every time you take it out of your pocket, you increase the chances of the unthinkable happening. Rings rarely get lost by themselves, and you could accidentally do something simple like put it in a different pocket or momentarily put it down on a chair or a pew.

The last thing you want is that ghastly dry-throat feeling of panic when you pat your pocket as the music strikes up, and realize that the ring is not where it should be. If a young attendant such as a pageboy is going to act as ring bearer and carry a ring cushion, make sure that someone responsible has been allocated to place the ring(s) on the cushion at the last possible moment. As you are likely to be up at the front with the groom, it may be a bit tricky time-wise for you to do it.

Blooming flowers

Alex Little, best man to Kieran O'Byrne, says: 'On the day, we drove to the venue early to make sure everything was organized,' says Alex. 'Kieran started to get nervous so I tried to calm him down by making light of the situation. I went down to the local pub and got us some lunch – food not liquid – because we suddenly realized we were starving. Just before the ceremony we discovered we had loads of buttonholes for the male guests but no one knew who to give them to. I turned to Kieran and he looked completely blank. He looked round for the bride who had ordered them and had drawn up a list, but she was about to make her entrance, so we had to ad lib it. It wasn't a panic really. Someone just said to me, "Who do you think is most important?" so we gave them to brothers, male family members and old friends. I think it worked in the end.'

AFTER THE CEREMONY
Leaving procession
Traditionally, the bridal couple are followed out by the groom's mum and the bride's dad, then the bride's mum and the groom's dad (or equivalent family members or partners), followed by the best man and the chief bridesmaid or matron of honour. The other bridesmaids or attendants bring up the rear. As soon as you have moved from the ceremony area to where everyone is gathering – whether it is for photos or just kissing and congratulating – ask the

ushers to check the church or ceremony room. In the excitement, this is when guests tend to leave behind cameras, gloves, glasses, confetti and all manner of things. It's much more difficult to retrieve lost items an hour later when the party may have moved to a different location, particularly as churches are often locked when not in use.

Directing the transport

With many stately homes and other venues now licensed for weddings, you may be lucky and find that the transition from ceremony to reception is merely a quick stroll through a rose garden. If so, you can skip this bit. If, however, 150 guests have to get across town on a Saturday afternoon, all your organizing skills will be called into play. Most guests will have already worked out how they will travel, or will have made arrangements for lifts, but don't count on it. This can be an awkward moment for someone on their own or from out of town. If there is no main transport laid on – some couples now hire a bus or even river boats to ferry guests from A to B – try to identify people who need a lift and flag down cars heading off half-empty. If you drove the groom to the ceremony, that's one extra seat in your car.

Clear directions

Invitations will often include a mini map or directions of how to get to the reception venue, which is a great piece of forward thinking. Unfortunately, with everything else to think about, you can't always trust guests to remember to bring them on the day. You can try driving off in convoy, but this usually falls down at the first set of traffic lights and because people have trouble identifying strangers' cars.

The best strategy is to keep a few spare maps or sets of directions in the glove compartment of your car, just in case. The chances are that all your guests will be sensible (and hopefully still sober) at this stage, and will be perfectly capable of getting themselves to another venue. These precautions are simply that – precautions. You only need one distant cousin to be stranded outside the church or register office because she popped to the loo to adjust her hat, and your neat schedule is already disrupted.

What a picture!

As with many wedding traditions, the photographs may not be styled in quite the same way as in previous generations. Some couples still go for the formal line-ups of family members outside the church or venue. However, some choose a much more fly-on-the-wall reportage style, where people are snapped chatting rather than posing for the camera. Other couples choose a mixture of both. Hopefully, you will be aware if any rounding-up of guests is needed at this stage. Confetti is not always allowed, particularly outside churches or register offices, so you may have to tactfully prevent an over-enthusiastic guest from emptying the contents of a confetti box over the happy couple.

Double as a pack horse

The groom may have lots of envelopes pressed into his hands throughout the day, and these often contain money or cheques. In all the excitement he may forget where he put them. As his right-hand man, offer to take care of them and either keep them in your own pockets or ask someone responsible (and sober!) to look after them. If the reception is at a hotel, you may be able to rent a safe-box for the day.

Checklist

- How are you getting to the groom's house if you haven't arranged to stay overnight?
- How are the two of you getting to the church/venue?
- How are you getting yourself to the reception when the groom goes off with the bride?
- How are you getting yourself and the couple home at the end of the party?
- Has your own car been serviced recently?
- Is the tank full, is it clean on the outside, clutter-free on the inside?
- Do you have plenty of change for parking meters?
- Have the ushers been fully briefed about orders of service, whether they are required to hand out buttonholes and to whom?
- Does someone (other than you) know to check the venue or church after the ceremony for gloves, cameras, etc?
- Has someone been appointed to wait around until all guests have clearly got lifts or some other form of transport to the reception?
- Do you have enough money if payments or fees need to be settled, eg the church or organist?

THE RECEPTION

'Always do sober what you said you'd do drunk.
That will teach you to keep your mouth shut.'
ERNEST HEMINGWAY

Arriving

There is a distinct shift of gear after the wedding ceremony and most of the principal players are usually noticeably less nervous. As best man you're now over halfway through your official duties. Hopefully, you've already got the groom to the ceremony on time, supervised the ushers and buttonholes, sung in tune, produced the rings at the necessary moment and got back down the aisle in one piece.

The couple are usually the first to leave the ceremony venue for the reception, followed by attendants and close family members. It's a good idea for someone to stay behind until everyone has gone, to make sure that no one has been stranded without a lift. Either take on this duty yourself, or, even better, nominate a reliable usher – preferably not someone too young or easily flustered. This will allow you enough time to get to the reception. Familiarize yourself with the layout there as soon as you can, if you have not been able to do so in advance. Guests will assume you know the location of everything from the ladies' toilet to the cigarette machine.

Safe place

Check that there is somewhere safe to display any presents that are brought by guests on the day. Even if the couple have arranged a gift-ordering service at a department store or through a specialist gift list company, there are always last-minute presents to be looked after, especially if extra guests are invited for the evening. Make sure that you look after envelopes full of vouchers or cash personally. In 2002, a hotel manageress in Sunderland was jailed after being found guilty of stealing cards from newlyweds too distracted at their receptions to notice they were missing. She was estimated to have pocketed more than £150,000 worth of cash and vouchers from unsuspecting wedding couples over a seven-year period. When she was arrested, she still had some of the cards with their personal messages which never reached their intended recipients.

Make yourself known

If you haven't already visited the venue with the couple prior to the wedding, introduce yourself to the party co-ordinator, *maître d'* or hotel manager as soon as you arrive. You should firmly impress upon them the importance of coming to you rather than the groom with any queries or problems. If something unforeseen does crop up, you can decide whether it's worth troubling him with it. This is also a good time to run through the rough timings with the venue staff – for instance, when guests will be seated and when the first course will be served. If there is a free bar, check the following details. Ask whether limits have been set as to what and how much is available; whether spirits are included and how the costs will be recorded. Ask for someone to let you know immediately when the money has run out.

A warm welcome

Most receptions start with some kind of drinks and nibbles, so keep a careful eye on the first and have plenty of the second. Champagne cocktails on an empty stomach are not the ideal ingredients for a clear head and a successful speech. Although many couples no longer bother with a formal receiving line, you may be required to accompany the bride and groom for a while, looking official and shaking hands. Don't worry if you can't think of anything wildly original or witty to say. Most of the guests won't know what to say either. The weather, the service and how beautiful the bride looks are fairly safe, if unimaginative, topics for small talk.

Seating plan

If the meal is seated, the top table traditionally comprises eight key figures.
From left to right they are:

◆ the chief bridesmaid
◆ the groom's father
◆ the bride's mother
◆ the groom
◆ the bride
◆ the bride's father
◆ the groom's mother
◆ the best man

This means you'll be seated next to the groom's mum. This can be great if you've known the groom for a long time, as you may well have known her for years, too. However, this will vary for each individual, depending on whether parents have remarried or been widowed. Increasingly, couples prefer not to have a top table, but sit among their friends and plan the rest of the seating so that their family are seated with other family members, rather than on display.

Master of ceremonies

If possible, study the seating plan in advance so that you know which table is which. No matter how clear the table plan, some guests will still come to you to ask where they are supposed to be sitting. If the venue provides a master of ceremonies, or the couple have booked a toastmaster, you will have got off lightly. If not, the best man is usually required to signal to guests when it is time to move into another room or take their seats, etc. The classic 'spoon on the side of a glass' routine is usually more successful than trying to shout over the hum of conversation.

Speak now!

It has become increasingly popular to have the speeches before the meal, so if this suggestion comes up during the wedding preparations, jump at the chance. This means that you can get the nerve-wracking bit out of the way early and gives you the opportunity to taste and enjoy your food. The cake is often cut at this stage, too – this means that the photographer can get the obligatory cake shot before packing up for the day and that one tier can be cut up to be served with the coffee.

Looking the part

Alex Little, best man to Kieran O'Byrne, says: 'You've got to be there for everybody – for the guests, the couple and, most importantly, the groom. I really enjoyed it, as you're focused all day long and guests all seem to know you. We did have a slight headache when two people turned up for the meal with partners even though it wasn't a plus-one invitation. We had to liaise with the catering staff and find somewhere for them to sit. It all worked out in the end because two other guests didn't come. You just have to shuffle tables around. People always ask the best man, "Do you mind if I swap with...?" as if you are in charge, and you just have to look like you know what you're doing.'

Keeping the peace

As the evening gathers pace, there is a possibility that some of the guests might abuse the couple's hospitality, and it may be necessary for the best man to put on his bouncer's hat. That's not to say you should start throwing guests off the premises, but if arguments break out or guests become unruly or incapable of standing, it's a good idea to move them outside to calm down or sober up.

It's at this stage that plans are often hatched to 'customize' the couple's room if they are staying on the premises or jazz up the car with boots, streamers or a mock ball and chain. Needless to say, no one should ever be allowed to tamper with the petrol tank, tyres or mechanics of a vehicle, so if the car is going to get the treatment, try to make sure it is a group activity so everyone can see exactly what is being done. The same thoughtfulness should also be given to the couple's bedroom.

Event co-ordinator Toni Henningsohn of Newmarket Weddings believes it is important to remember the newlyweds' need for privacy. 'Although the best man is often seen as the instigator of "decorating" the couple's room, I think it's important to keep guests away,' she says. 'It's best to talk to the bride and groom first and say, "Look, if the ushers/guests/old friends approach me and suggest something, what do you want me to do? Do you want me to put them off?". This actually gives the couple the chance to have a say in what happens. Some ideas are quite sweet and nice and others are totally way out and it's best not to go there.'

Have you got it covered?

- Do you know the name of the contact at the reception (manager, *maître d'*, etc.)?
- Is there enough space for coats?
- Is there somewhere to display any gifts brought along on the day?
- Is there somewhere safe to lock away gifts of cash?
- Are you required to be master of ceremonies?
- Does the number of tables and chairs correspond to the number of guests?
- Do you have your speech or your notes with you?
- Do you have the number of a reliable taxi service for the end of the night?

UNACCUSTOMED AS I AM...

*'The human brain is a wonderful thing. It starts
working the moment you are born and never stops
until you stand up to speak in public!'*
SIR GEORGE JESSEL

Tell anyone you're going to be a best man and the first thing they will mention is the dreaded speech. If you're someone who has done little, if any, public speaking, the fear of doing so can prey on your mind for months. Wedding consultant Kerry Johnson of Happily Hitched recalls one best man who just couldn't face it on the day. 'He was desperately shy and unaccustomed to public speaking,' she says. 'When it came to the lull when the coffee was being served and the speeches were about to start, he was nowhere to be found. So great was his fear of giving a speech that he'd actually left the wedding. Luckily, the groom's other brother stepped in to deliver an impromptu performance.'

Scared to death!

'According to an American study, glossophobia, or fear of public speaking, is top of the list of people's fears, ahead of arachnophobia (fear of spiders) and even the fear of death,' says voice coach Karen Malim, who runs workshops in communications skills. 'An American study in the 1960s showed the impact a speaker makes is 55% body language, 38% voice and 7% content. The decision of an audience to listen is based not on logic, but on instinct – a direct emotional response to the body language, eye contact, vocal power and tone of the speaker.' And you thought it was just about scribbling down a few well-chosen words and mumbling through them as best you could!

Best men are usually chosen because they are relatives or old friends of the groom, rather than for their ability to fascinate 200 guests with seamless witty prose. For any prospective best man, the most important thing to remember is that you are standing up in front of people who share a love of the couple, hope the day will be a success and want you to do well. Plus, they will have had a couple of drinks by the time you stand up and will, you hope, be in a forgiving mood. Expect heckles and laughter, especially from friends, but take this as a positive reaction to your efforts, not a deliberate ploy to put you off. Once you get into your stride you can often use these interruptions and heckles for a little off-the-cuff spontaneity.

The main ingredients

Your speech should do all or most of the following:

♦ Wish the bride and groom a happy future together.
♦ Thank the groom for asking you to be best man.
♦ Tell funny stories about the groom.
♦ Talk a little about the bride.
♦ Thank the bride on behalf of the bridesmaids.
♦ Thank the hosts on behalf of the guests.

When to speak

The blind panic of having to speak in public has ruined many a wedding day for the principal players. That is why it has become increasingly popular to break with convention and have the speeches at the beginning of or early on in the reception. Traditionally, they come after the meal while the cake is being sliced and handed round, which can mean waiting until quite late into the evening. By getting the speeches out of the way earlier, the groom, best man and bride's dad can relax and enjoy their food without that dry-throat feeling of dread. It also means that guests who may not know people's names will feel a little more familiar with the speakers at the top table and consequently, more at home. Having the speeches before the meal also gives guests who don't know each other something extra to chat about.

Looking for inspiration

What to say? Obviously you want to make your mark, rather than sound like the thousands of best men who have gone before you, but there is a fine line between being original and being obscure. For five heart-stopping minutes you need to appeal to a variety of generations and backgrounds. In-jokes are simply not going to work, as they quickly alienate entire tables. It is also important to keep the focus on the bride and groom as a couple, rather than dwelling on your shared history with the groom, no matter how far back you and he go. Having said that, going right back in time for little anecdotes is often a safe bet. Harmless tales of childhood and early school days are usually sweet and inoffensive. If you want to move into the college or university years, be sure of your territory, in case you unwittingly stray into a sensitive area involving exes.

Coping with nerves

Eat. It's a simple but vital precaution. Make sure you have something at breakfast and at lunchtime if the wedding is in the afternoon. Food will not only quell any nausea (common for someone riddled with nerves) but those first couple of swift drinks at the reception will go straight into your bloodstream on an empty stomach. In no time you could look flushed and even a little unsteady on your feet. Even if you normally hold your drink well, alcohol can affect you quite differently when the adrenalin is pumping. Try to make a little Dutch courage go a long way. You can knock back the bubbly in celebration after the speech.

Voice coach Karen Malim trained at the Royal Academy of Music and still performs as a singer, so she is well versed in the art of overcoming stage fright. 'You're in good company if you feel butterflies and need to run to the bathroom more often than usual,' she says. 'Barbra Streisand didn't sing live for many years after she fluffed her words at a concert in New York and Laurence Olivier used to feel so sick with fear before his great Shakespearean roles, he had to have an understudy waiting in the wings. A little bit of anxiety is helpful as it gives an edge to a performance.' But just to ensure that your performance is not too 'edgy' Karen recommends the tips on the following page.

Combat stage fright

◆ Try this actor's technique for deflecting fear and anxiety. Push a wall with one leg in front of the other. Stand a foot or so in front of a wall and push it for all you're worth. Change legs and hands and repeat.

◆ Relaxation and meditation. Tapes can be very useful, as can visual imagery. Picture a perfect speech in the present tense. The end result is exactly as you wish it to be, so focus on that.

◆ Cut back on caffeine and alcohol. Both dehydrate you and alcohol dulls the senses, lulling you into a false sense of security about your performance.

◆ Avoid dairy products near the wedding date. They produce mucous which could adversely affect your vocal strength and clarity.

◆ Don't gargle if you have a sore throat. This will inflame the vocal cords. Instead, inhale steam (without any additives) to lubricate the voice.

◆ Clean your teeth. A clean mouth is a happy mouth.

◆ All for one. Think of your audience as a single entity rather than a sea of individuals.

Content

It seems to be an unwritten rule that the best man refers to some wildly outrageous but secret carry-on from the stag night, at which point all those who went to the stag night collapse into fits of knowing laughter (despite having little recollection of what went on) while everyone else smiles nervously. This may seem a little trite but it could be expected of you, so check with the happy couple whether they want the traditional 'what-a-lads'-night-out-that-was' approach. If, on the other hand, you all went off for a relaxing golf weekend, resist reading out all the scores and handicaps.

Don't go there

Scriptwriter and speech writer Malcolm Perkins of www.wantaspeech.co.uk is not a fan of raking over the stag night coals and advises caution. 'The best man's speech should never be regarded as an extension of the stag night,' he says. 'It will not go down well with the family audience and you will probably be the one who is embarrassed.' Only you know how tales of trousers around ankles and vomiting in cabs will go down, but remember that all the people in the room will find different things funny. Received wisdom also states that you should be very careful about including the subjects listed opposite in a best man's speech.

- Jokes – unless you are very good at telling them.
- In-jokes – as already mentioned, and three-quarters of the guests won't get them anyway.
- Rude words or innuendo – you could ruin the whole day for an over-sensitive mum or granny.
- Swear words – come on, it's only five minutes. Choose from the millions of other words in the English language.
- Ex-lovers or former spouses – even if the bride or groom think it's funny, it may embarrass families or children from these previous unions.

I'm not naturally funny

Even if you are not a born comic, speech writer Malcolm Perkins suggests you try to put a couple of witty one-liners at the beginning of your speech. 'It will give you confidence to receive a laugh,' he says. 'Unless you are a good joke teller, I would stay away from long jokes. When you are nervous, it is far easier to deliver a one-liner. There are websites where you can find wedding-related jokes. Just go to your favourite search engine and ask for "wedding humour". Some of the jokes might be mildly suggestive, but would probably be acceptable in a best man's speech. Just tread carefully and if you are unsure, pick another.'

Such a card

It is traditionally the best man's job to read telegrams from absent family or friends, although e-mails are increasingly taking their place. Don't try to read all the cards and messages, especially the ones that just say 'Best wishes' and are from people at the reception. Frankly, it can get very dull and you are almost bound to end up leaving out one very important godmother. Try to grab two minutes with the groom or bride beforehand to run through which are the most significant and edit them down. There may also be some personal messages which the couple would prefer not to have read aloud.

Scene-stealers

Props can be a great ice-breaker. Old childhood photos blown up on a piece of card always get an 'Ahh!' but be sure to include the bride as well as the groom. You may need to liaise with one of her friends or bridesmaids for a photo. Ask someone of the bride's own age rather than her mum, if possible, as a friend is more likely to be in tune with what the bride would find funny and what she would find embarrassing. Think about how or where the couple met – on holiday, skiing, at a football match, at work or whatever – and bring along a few comic props wrapped in ribbon. Don't, however, turn it into a Cecil B De Mille production with complicated sets and scenery that obviously took you weeks. It may be well meant, but some guests might feel that you are trying to steal the show.

Delivery

Don't rush it. There is no rewind button on this occasion and if you set off at breakneck speed, people will start whispering, 'What did he say?' and look quizzically at each other. You will go down in history as the best man nobody could hear. Many venues provide some form of amplifier, especially in the increasingly popular large halls in stately homes. Find out about this in advance and try to get in a little practice first. Nothing is more embarrassing than watching someone clearly at a loss in front of a microphone, speaking too closely, bending uncomfortably or causing wince-inducing feedback. To help you get a perfect delivery, voice coach Karen Malim has written an e-book called VoicePOWER, which is available via her website www.centerstagetraining.com. She recommends that you tape yourself reading a passage from a book and listen for the points listed overleaf.

- Pace. Are you a speed speaker or slow and deliberate? Practise different speeds until you find a happy medium.
- Articulation. Do you let one word run into another, eg 'let us pray' becomes 'lettuce spray'?
- Falling line. If your sentences fade out at the end, you are throwing away your impact.
- Vocal range. Do you vary the pitch so it has some music in it, or does it lack interest because it is monotone? Try imagining that you are reading a child a story. Even reading boring instructions in this way can make them seem interesting.
- Repetition. Do you fall prey to verbal viruses such as 'um', 'uh' and meaningless phrases such as 'like' and 'you know'? Replace them with a pause.
- Resonance. This is using your vocal mechanism to amplify your voice without strain. Pretend you can smell something unpleasant and you will notice your nostrils dilate. What also happens is that your soft palate tightens, just like the skin of a drum, creating a more effective surface for the sound of your voice to bounce off.
- Projection. By placing the words further forward in the mouth you make them brighter and more audible. You can practise this with the 'big chew' which will free the jaw and help you to feel the

sound vibrations at the front of your palate. Chew
as though you were eating a tough steak and then
add sound: 'ah-mm-ng-ee-ah-mm-ng', and so on.
Feel the vibrations towards the front of the mouth.
Now say words with vowels that are made
towards the front of the mouth such as bean, mean,
seen, hen and bed, noticing what that feels like.
Follow this with words that are made nearer the
rear of the mouth and put them at the front where
the bright vowels are made, eg car, far, boot, book,
cot. This is voice projection.

Ask an expert

This is often a good option. In the title role of the film
The Wedding Planner, Jennifer Lopez stands innocently
at the back of a reception wearing a Madonna mike
and whispering the best man's speech to him through
an ear-piece. When rumbled by an amazed guest, she
quickly replies, 'What? You think Kissinger came up
with his own stuff?' Perhaps being fed a speech is
taking things a little far, but it makes sense to take
professional advice.

'The temptation is usually to go on too long,' says
Keith Anderson of Crisp and Cheerful Speeches, who
has been writing personalized prose for grooms and
best men for twelve years. 'It's best to keep a speech to

five minutes maximum. You don't need to be afraid of public speaking inasmuch as you're not appearing in court, you're not being accused of anything and you don't need to persuade anyone about anything.

'The thing that most grooms, fathers-of-the-bride and best men don't like to do is rehearse, but this is the only way you can get to the point where you can stand up, look your guests in the eye and give the impression that you're making it up as you go along. People love a speaker to look nonchalant, not glued to his notes.

'A rule of thumb is to rehearse one hour for each minute of your speech. So a five-minute speech needs five hours' rehearsal, although not necessarily all at once, preferably with a tape recorder. That way you can pick up your mistakes. It sounds very boring but you will seem more confident when you stand up, maybe even enough to try a little ad-libbing. If someone is still eating, for instance, you can try quips like "when you get to the white part, that's the plate", although you may not get away with it if the wedding is very formal.

'Don't forget, while you're rehearsing you read your own speech dozens of times but the audience only hears it once. In other words, don't rush. If you speak slowly and deliberately, people are more likely to remember what you have said.'

Shaky start

Alex Little gave a speech at the wedding of his friend Kieran O'Byrne. 'I was nervous about the speech which I wrote about two days before the wedding,' he says. 'I kept it nice and short and didn't try to be funny. I wanted to be sincere rather than entertaining. I did practise reading it out to my flatmate, which helped, but it's better once you've got an audience. When you are saying it to the right people, it flows a lot more easily. Reading it to a mirror seems stale and cold and you're not sure how it's going to go down. In context it's a lot more fun and you can even start to improvise. I wish I'd actually learned part of it, though, as my hands were full of pieces of paper and when you start shaking, it really shows.'

Need a hand?

Your stance and what you do with your hands can bolster your confidence. People will notice if you shuffle from foot to foot. Standing with your hands in your pockets is a bit casual and holding them behind your back will make you look like Prince Philip. Hold your prompt cards even if you don't need them, because it gives you something to do with your hands, or hold guests' cards and telegrams. Never lean on your hands. Your speech should end with a toast, so make sure you have a glass nearby and that it still has something in it, even if it's only a mouthful.

Body language

Karen Malim, of Centre Stage Training, likens the human body to an instrument and offers this advice:

- ◆ Give your body a stable base with feet shoulder-width apart and weight evenly distributed over the soles of the feet.
- ◆ Keep your knees unlocked like an animal waiting to pounce or a tennis player waiting to receive a serve.
- ◆ Keep your head and neck in alignment by imagining you are being held by your ears – this lengthens the spine and neck and allows the vocal apparatus to do its work freely.
- ◆ Check your jaw is unclamped – you don't want to sound like a ventriloquist.
- ◆ Don't slump. It drains your energy and will make you appear unenthusiastic. Imagine you see through eyes that are situated in the chest just below the collar bone. This will give you an air of authority and make you stand up to your full height.
- ◆ Don't confuse this with an army-style ramrod back which will block the energy flow and make you appear wooden.

- Lean forward to emphasize a point as though you are confiding in an audience. Barristers do this when they are talking to juries.
- Facial expression is an important tool. Practise the vowel sounds 'oo-ee-oo-ee' in an exaggerated way until you feel all your face muscles working. Don't forget to smile.

Order of speakers

There may be a toastmaster or master of ceremonies at the reception venue. If not, the task will probably fall to you. The usual order of speakers is as follows:

1. The father-of-the-bride
(or close relative or family friend in his place)

The bride's father opens the speeches by saying a few words of welcome and thanks. If he is nervous or a first-time speaker, he might well make a comment about the weather, so try to steer away from the obvious in your own speech. He may also say something along the lines of, 'I'm not losing a daughter but gaining a son'. It may be a cliché but it is heart-felt so, as best man, try to encourage laughter and a ripple of applause. The father-of-the-bride usually concludes by proposing a toast to the newlyweds.

2. The groom

Although he is 'man of the match' in every other respect, it is not usually the role of the groom to give a wildly funny or urbane speech – if anyone is going to have them rolling in the aisles, it's the best man. The groom needs to be romantic, genuine and adoring towards his new bride. The groom replies to the bride's father on behalf of his new wife and compliments the bridesmaids, proposing a toast to them.

3. The bride

It is increasingly popular for brides to stand up and speak for themselves and this is usually the point at which they do it. Be aware of the bride's plans and make sure she doesn't have to shout you back down into your seat in your enthusiasm to get started.

4. The best man

The best man replies on behalf of the bridesmaids and winds up proceedings with his speech – this should be no more than five minutes unless you have the wit and linguistic skills of Stephen Fry. Now is the time to read out selected cards, telegrams or e-mails.

TOP 10 CHECKLIST

Think carefully about these crucial points from speech writer Malcolm Perkins:

1. Reading straight from the page

If you go for this option, which is obviously the easiest, read through your speech as many times as possible before the event. It is best to read it out aloud, as if you are giving the speech. You will have a lot more confidence on the day if you are familiar with your speech.

2. Learning it off by heart

This is the hard option, but if you have a good memory it is worth a try. Unless you have a brilliant memory, have the back-up of a few key words written on paper or cards. This way, if you stumble you have a prompt to get you flowing again. It's not easy giving the speech off by heart and if you do dry up, finding where you left off on the script can be tricky. Therefore choose either option 1 or option 2, not a combination.

3. Smile

A witty speech needs to be given in a tongue-in-cheek manner with a smile in your voice. It won't seem anywhere near as funny if your voice is flat.

4. Go for laughs

Try to open the speech with a witty comment. Once you have got your first laugh, you will feel much more confident.

5. React to your audience

Listen out for appreciative laughter and let it die down before carrying on.

6. Don't state the obvious

Try not to say that you are nervous. Everybody assumes you are anyway. Your speech will seem so much more professional if you don't labour this point.

7. Exude confidence

When you stand up, you'll probably receive a round of applause. Hold your head up in the air, look around the room and give everybody a big smile. This makes people think you are relaxed, and relaxes them. When making a toast, make your announcement very positive. Wait until everybody is standing. Lift your glass confidently into the air and wait until everyone has lifted their glasses before giving the toast.

8. Watch your eyeline

It is far better to look at people than at a piece of paper. If you are reading your speech, hold it up in the air and look over the top as many times as you can. If your hands are shaking, rest the paper on a flat surface.

9. Embrace your emotions

Try to make the serious bits sound sincere. Some men are not happy at being thought of as sincere or 'soppy'. A wedding is a loving occasion and your street cred will remain just the same, regardless of how romantically you refer to people. In fact, it might even improve.

10. Don't doubt yourself

The more times you read over your speech, the less funny it will seem. Self-doubt will creep in and you may feel like altering or deleting some parts. This is normal. Remember, if you found the speech funny the first time you read it, that is how others will find it the first time they hear it.

AFTER THE PARTY'S OVER

'Laugh and the world laughs with you, snore
and you sleep alone.'
ANTHONY BURGESS

Well done, you did it! Now fix yourself a large Alka
Seltzer and reflect on the day. Even if things didn't go
exactly according to plan, there is a good chance that
no one noticed. In any case, people will not hold you
personally responsible (unless, of course, you got
blind drunk before your speech or tried to chat up
someone with a partner present, in which case you're
on your own, pal!).

Keep on dancing

In previous years, couples would change into what
was called their 'going away' clothes, kiss everyone
goodbye, throw the bouquet and drive off to their
honeymoon before the end of the reception. But who
wants to leave the biggest – and most expensive –
party of their lives before the last glass has been
emptied? Most modern couples prefer to stay until
the end of the evening and leave their honeymoon
departure until the next day or even the one after that.
For the best man, this takes the pressure off having to

look after passports and tickets and arranging transport to the airport along with everything else.

It also avoids the problem of the reception losing momentum when the leading players disappear. In the classic *Four Weddings And A Funeral*, Hugh Grant's character Charles tries to tempt Andie MacDowell back to the marquee after the newlyweds have left with the line, 'the evening's only just started'. 'I think we both know that's a lie,' she quips back. So with the pressure of getting the couple to the airport lifted from the best man's shoulders, what happens next?

The morning after

There may be a get-together brunch or lunch the day after the wedding, where close friends and family relive the highlights, open presents or watch amateur videos. If something like this has been arranged, as best man you will no doubt be invited (unless you are still blushing over misdemeanours alluded to earlier). If you were asked to look after any money or cheques given to the couple at the reception, now is the time to ask the bride or groom what they want done with them. You could offer to pay the cheques into the bank for them while they are away; but frankly, the contents of the envelopes are a private matter, so they may prefer not to disclose this, even to you. It's probably best to hand the envelopes back to them and discharge your duty as soon as possible. The couple may want the cash to take on holiday with them anyway.

Officially, you've more or less done your bit now, so take the opportunity at any follow-up gathering to enjoy yourself, relax and bask in the warm praise that you will inevitably receive for your sparkling speech (see previous chapter). However, there may be a few outstanding jobs to be done over the next few days, and, if everything has been organized properly, you will already be up to speed on these.

Disposable cameras

If you were deemed reliable and sober enough to be entrusted with the couple's precious memories, you may now find yourself in charge of the disposable cameras left on tables at the reception. Get these processed at the earliest opportunity so there is no danger of them getting lost. If you're taking them to a chemist or photographic shop and the couple have gone on honeymoon, put the counterfoils in a safe place and keep them there until the couple return.

The newlyweds will want to see the photographs before anyone else. If the pictures go into general circulation before the bride and groom come back, not only does it spoil the surprise for the honeymooners but guests caught in funny poses or varying degrees of inebriation may try to start editing them. There may also be some particularly compromising or embarrassing pictures of family members which the bride and groom may want to censor.

Hired suits

The bride's mother, sister or bridesmaid will be responsible for dry cleaning and storing the wedding dress, but any hired morning suits will need to be returned – usually the first working day after the wedding. If ushers or other key players in the groom's party hired their clothes locally where they live, then it is their responsibility to get them back in one piece. If, however, the suits all came from one outlet, try to arrange for them all to be dropped off together, or at least delivered to your home so that you can check everything off and establish whether there is any damage. Don't attempt to sponge or clean any marks or sew up any rips or tears. Most hire companies will have charged you a nominal fee – usually a couple of pounds – for accidental damage cover when you took out the outfit, so unless the suit is completely trashed, you should be okay.

Money matters

If there has been some serious damage to hired outfits or the top hat is lost, for instance, and there is a charge or loss of deposit, initially you may have to cough up. If it was your suit, it is basically your responsibility. If it was the groom's, keep details and receipts and make a mental note to sort it out with him later. There may be other unforeseen expenses on the day which you will have settled on behalf of the couple – last-minute taxis, tips for waiting staff, and topping up the float behind the bar. Don't make money the first thing you mention to the groom after the honeymoon, but don't feel that you have to absorb extra costs either, unless it is such a small amount it is not worth mentioning. The groom won't want you to be out of pocket because of his wedding.

All present and correct

Contingency plans should have been made for looking after any presents brought to the reception. Increasingly, modern couples are placing their wedding list with a gift list company or department store and delivery will have been arranged directly by them, usually to coincide with their return from honeymoon. But some guests always bring something along on the day, especially if they are only coming to the evening party. If you arranged to have gifts locked up for safe-keeping at the hotel where the reception was held, go and retrieve them as soon as possible.

You may find that there are a lot of presents which will need storing until the couple's return. If you are responsible for keeping them safe, check your home contents insurance policy, or give your insurer a quick call. Think twice before volunteering to be guardian of the gifts if you are out at work all day every day. It might be better for them to be kept at a house where people are around during the day. Thieves are canny and it is quite easy for them to spot you packing a load of presents in the back of the car then to follow you home to see where you live.

Thanks for everything

In return for your months of support, encouragement and hand-holding, it's quite likely that the couple will give you a gift. A short note thanking them is a nice way to round off the wedding. Don't just buy a standard 'thank you' card and sign it 'from Andy' or whatever. Try to write a few, well-chosen lines about how much you really enjoyed the experience (you did, you did!) and make it personal and worth keeping for years to come.

Have you remembered?

- Disposable cameras – who's got them? Who should have them?
- Presents – who's looking after them and are they adequately insured?
- Have all the hire suits gone back to the outfitters?
- Do you have all the receipts for any extra costs you personally incurred on the day?
- Do you have a contact number for the couple on honeymoon, just in case?
- Is someone collecting the couple from the airport? Having to get on a train after the honeymoon of a lifetime is a bit of an anti-climax.

NOW THAT'S WHAT I CALL A STAG NIGHT!

*'I've had hangovers before, but this time
even my hair hurts.'*
ROCK HUDSON IN *PILLOW TALK*

Where to choose?

In soap operas, characters rarely go further than the Rovers Return or the Queen Vic for a few pints, some saucy banter and a kebab on the way home, but in real life, stag parties have become increasingly ambitious. Many grooms take the view that they can get drunk and have a meal out any day of the year, so opt for an adventure/activity weekend.

Richard Kaffel has not only been to a few stag parties himself, as a participant and as best man, but also as director of event and experience company Red Letter Days. He offers more than 300 experiences from adrenalin-pumping activities to relaxation weekends, so he knows quite a bit about what lads like to do when they get together.

Something really different

'There has definitely been a move away from the standard pub, club and curry tradition,' he says. 'We still find elements of this remain, but I think guys are a bit more PC nowadays. They don't want to have to tell their mates and girlfriend that they've just been to a lap-dancing club. Obviously, there are some people who, however much effort you go to, still actually just want to go and get drunk, but it's becoming less common.

'Certainly the stag night is more likely to be a night and a day or even a weekend. One of my theories is that it's because men are marrying older so they've already experienced more. Many grooms have done corporate entertainment days and team-building events. They've been there, seen it, done it. Some guys say to us "Actually, I've done quad biking with my company, now I want something really different". That's when experiences such as tank driving or SAS training come in. At the end of the day, when you've got twenty or thirty guys all muddied up in army uniforms, you can get some great pictures to tell the story for the speeches. With this sort of spirit of adventure in mind, we also launched a fire-fighter course and a lifeboat training experience where you basically go down to the south coast, throw someone overboard and then rescue him. No prizes for guessing who gets thrown in!'

With many adventurous activities, however, drinking – the traditional staple of the stag party – is a no-no. 'None of these things involves alcohol and it's a serious point,' stresses Richard. 'If guys have been up drinking until the early hours, they may be stopped from doing certain activities because safety comes first. All the driving events, for instance, will have things such as Breathalysers on the day. It might be taking place on private land, but when there are other people around and marshals everywhere, it's too dangerous to take risks.'

Can people afford it?

Presumably, as best man you know the groom well enough to establish whether his fancy is more easily tickled by paint balling or a stripper bearing baby oil, but it never pays to assume anything. When you're in charge of organizing a stag do, always plan it with the groom in mind, not based on what you want, or the potential for a cheap laugh during the speeches. If the groom has said he wants to go away to a European city for a weekend, or to Portugal for a golf tournament, think carefully about the cost implications. Some of the guys he would like to invite to the stag party may not be able to afford it, especially if they are already shelling out for a present and a new suit.

Red light warning

When Jason Hall was best man to old school friend Darren, the groom had very definite ideas about the sort of stag weekend he wanted Jason to help him organize.

'He really wanted to go to Amsterdam for the weekend – not for the reason that most people think! – but just to soak up the atmosphere of the coffee bars, so we got a party of five together. On the Saturday we said, "Right, it's your day, what do you want to do?" and he said he wanted to visit a museum. So we strolled off to Amsterdam's main museum and had a nice cultured morning. We had lunch, had a few drinks throughout the day and took in the sights – especially of all the other stag groups that were around us! It was unbelievable what some of them were getting up to.

'The biggest party was a load of young guys in their very early twenties wearing football shirts with their names on the back. Out hotel was pretty close to the red-light district and we kept seeing this same group milling about everywhere getting drunker and drunker. Eventually they bombarded this one particular small brothel and threw two or three of the guys inside. You could see them through the windows, inside the rooms, going "We're in, we're in!". A couple of us would have quite liked to go to a red-light district show out of curiosity, because it's something we've never done, but the groom really didn't want that to be part of the remit, which is fair enough because it was his weekend.

'It was a fantastic laugh though. We had the most appalling digs – like a nuclear bunker with no air, no windows, no air-conditioning. It wasn't cheap, either. It was a normal hotel near the centre of town which we looked up on the Internet and it seemed okay. As there were only five of us, we thought we'd take a group room together and have a laugh, which we did, but it was a very hot laugh. I can only describe the room as like a Vietcong dugout. There we were in our bunks, joking that at any moment an American soldier was going to come up through the floor like a scene from an Oliver Stone film and point a gun at us! Due to finances, a few old friends couldn't make the Amsterdam weekend, so I organized a night at the dog racing track for them the following weekend.

'A few months later I was best man again, this time to a mate who was actually having the ceremony in the Seychelles, but was holding a party like a reception when they came back. As this guy is an actor and a friend of ours was in a West End musical, we all went to see that and for a meal afterwards.'

I'm getting married in the morning

Planning a stag party the night before the wedding is a very bad idea. This leaves no time for the groom (and everyone else) to recover properly, especially if the affair is organized along traditional alcohol-fuelled lines. What's more, it's likely that the groom will have other last-minute arrangements to make or family to see. So, even before you know exactly what form the stag party may take, pencil in a couple of possible weekends early on. This is especially important if the wedding is in the summer, when key friends and family start planning holidays.

Who should be included?

Only you and the groom can answer that. Fathers and older relatives often don't want to join in with anything too boisterous or activity based, and may be quite satisfied with a pint down the pub the night before the wedding. Richard Kaffel of Red Letter Days increasingly finds that groups of men are planning their stag weekends to tie in with the bride and her girlfriends.

'It's not so much a joint thing, but on the Saturday the girls will maybe go off for a health spa day and the guys will go motor racing nearby, then on the Sunday they will all meet up and go out for a nice lunch together,' he says. For the really adventurous, Red Letter Days can even arrange a Sex School experience offering a girls' session, a guys' session and a mixed session.

High jinks

Footballer-turned-actor Vinnie Jones chose to go to Cork for his stag do. He took sixty-two mates, including his dad and Wimbledon manager Joe Kinnear, for a weekend of drinking, card schools and leg-pulling. Admittedly, the hotel manager had to stop some of them from jumping in the river from the bridge and risking treacherous currents! 'There was a group of police with dogs when we arrived back at Stansted,' Jones writes in *Vinnie: The Autobiography* (£6.99 Headline). 'They must have been warned there was a boisterous party of lads flying in but there was no trouble. They joined in the crack, managing to smile while the rest of us collapsed as some of the lads squatted, motionless, on the luggage carousel as it went round and round, through the exit flaps and back again.'

A safe pair of hands

Jones's agent had sold the exclusive pictures of his stag party to a tabloid newspaper, but your job as best man is to keep your groom – clothed or not – out of the headlines. There's usually at least one loony among the party who thinks it would be a hilarious idea to strip the groom, cover him with itching powder and tie him to a lamppost; however, as best man you may have to step in and be the party-pooper.

Sadly, there is always the chance that something could go tragically wrong. One best man recalls the horror of a pub crawl around London's fashionable St Katharine's Dock by Tower Bridge. A few over-excited members of the party thought it would be a laugh to jump in the Thames and swim across the opening to the dock. One or two even began to drag the inebriated groom towards the dock edge. It was only after much white-faced pleading and the firm intervention of the best man that the hapless groom was allowed to get back onto his wobbly legs and walk to safety. At the time, they labelled him a 'wuss'. The truth of the matter – as they discovered later – was that the groom couldn't swim, even when stone-cold sober.

'No-nos' on a booze-fuelled stag night

◆ Don't leave the groom stranded at the end of the night if he has drunk too much. See him indoors and try to make him drink a large glass of water.

- Never allow any pranks involving a razor. Beards and moustaches will not grow back in a week and grooms with one eyebrow look positively possessed.
- If strippers, lap dancers or semi-clad singing telegrams are involved and the groom looks obviously embarrassed, don't let things go too far.
- Watch for anyone taking compromising pictures. The bride may have a serious sense of humour failure if they do the rounds later at the reception.

No ritual humiliation

When Bob Wheeler was best man to Julian, he suggested a long weekend in Cornwall. 'I did all the legwork and the bookings, although I arranged it with Julian's knowledge and we worked on it together,' he says. 'There were about twelve of us in three caravans on a campsite. None of us surfs but we'd heard you could do that there, so we treated it as a cheap alternative to going away. We managed to do some surfing – more belly boarding really – and had a go at paintballing. I came up with the idea initially, because I know what Julian and most of us are like and we really would cringe at anything approaching one of those stripper-type stag nights. We tried to do something that got everyone together and would be great fun without having to go through the ritual humiliation process.'

You decide

So what would events supremo Richard Kaffel – a bachelor at the time of going to press – like for his own stag celebrations should the big day ever come? 'Probably something that involved a few different activities,' he concludes. 'When I was a best man, I organized a guys' weekend in Edinburgh. We stayed in this haunted house and on the Friday night put on some great visual effects, such as smoke coming out of people's rooms. On the Saturday we did quad biking, tank driving and 4x4 driving, then on the Sunday we did shooting and falconry, which was a nice way to wind down the weekend.

'I think I'd quite fancy some Ferrari driving and some tank driving. The key thing to remember is that you're getting together a load of people who may not know each other very well. Some might be work mates, university friends or guys from the Sunday morning football team. Getting them out and doing something is usually more effective at breaking the ice than sitting them all round a table.'

HELP, I NEED SOMEBODY

'I think men who have a pierced ear are better prepared for marriage. They've experienced pain and bought jewellery.'
RITA RUDNER

You don't have to be a complete wedding expert to find the right weekend activity for the stag night or hire the correct suit, you just have to do a little research. This may be the one occasion, for instance, where you don't buy your shirt from the high street or do need a little help with the one-liners in your speech. Not everyone is a natural Jack Dee. Whatever your requirements, there are thousands of suppliers, shops and websites that can help you in your quest and every issue of *You & Your Wedding* is packed with advice, stockists and wedding professionals to set you on your way. On the next few pages are just some of those who might be able to help.

Happily Hitched (07951-577782)
www.happilyhitched.com

A wedding planning service that offers tips on writing a speech and organizing a stag night. The new grooms' package includes a returns service so no one needs to worry about getting those suits back to the shop and will also advise the groom and best man on buying gifts.

Newmarket Wedding Service (01223-307300)
www.newmarketweddings.co.uk

Wedding co-ordination service operating in the south-east, East Anglia and the Midlands.

www.confetti.co.uk (0870-840 6060)

Another comprehensive website offering an interesting section on men's wear, with tips and style predictions from leading designers. There's a section on stag parties, including hangover cures and stag nights from hell.

www.kodakweddings.co.uk (0800-783 7452)
As the name suggests, this is a good port of call for
throwaway cameras and photographic needs, but it is
also a one-stop shop with thousands of wedding
suppliers and professionals in the UK. Key in your
location and what you require, eg formal wear hire,
and your nearest suppliers will come up, complete
with directions and a mileage count.

www.weddingguide.co.uk (020-7428 8373)
Good for grooming and speech advice, this site reveals
the interesting fact that the best man's role dates
back to a time when grooms stole their brides, so the
best man had to be a good scrapper!

STAG PARTIES

www.blackpoolstagnights.co.uk (01253-400236)
Offers a wide selection of hotels specifically catering
for stag nights with pre-arranged VIP passes to
nightclubs.

Red Letter Days (0870-444 7000/4004)
www.redletterdays.co.uk
Offers lots of suggestions for groups looking for an
activity, from sex appeal and nostalgia weekends to
anything using water, wheels or wings. There's even
an SAS-style survival course. Mix-and-match
weekends can be tailor-made and venues can be
found all over the UK.

www.stagweekends.com (0870-240 3746)
A user-friendly and practical lads' site with a database
of activities offering everything from assault courses
to yachting. Accommodation is graded 1 (no
misbehaving allowed here!) to 3 (bomb proof!) and
there's a chance to experience or submit 'interesting'
photos from stag weekends gone by.

www.callofthewild.co.uk (01639-700388)
An eclectic selection of short-break and weekend
packages, from pampering and health and fitness to
paragliding, kayaking and clay pigeon shooting. All-in
deals even include alcohol.

www.eclipseleisure.com (01273-727333)
A selection of club/accommodation deals tailored for
stag groups in Edinburgh, Brighton, Newcastle,
Manchester, Nottingham and Bournemouth. Packages
include nightclubs, lap-dancing clubs, comedy stores
and theme bars.

www.thestagdo.com
A comprehensive site offering the best man a free
organizer tool to help arrange the do, contact the
participants and share photos afterwards.

www.partyparties.co.uk (01442-834993)
Offers a venues database and a tool to create invitations,
plus a wide selection of custom-made parties from
nightclubbing on a party bus to stand-up comedy
evenings.

www.senorstag.com (020-7900 2479)
Short-break packages to Barcelona, which can include a
bit of Barcelona FC, fiesta, go-karting, paintballing, bike
rides and even chauffeur-driven transportation.

www.toptable.co.uk (0870-850 8454)
Free booking service for restaurants in London, Paris and thirty cities across the UK, including some of the 'unbookable' restaurants. Specify stag party and type in the number in the party and suggestions will come up online.

www.ianwrightorg.com (01732-529511)
The Ian Wright Organization based in Kent organizes everything from off-road racing to sumo wrestling and team tasks.

TRAVEL

www.i-escape.com
Discount online booking service for hideaway hotels.

Hotels Booking Service (020-7437 5052)
Nationwide hotel-booking service.

www.deckchair.com
Easy-to-use site with cheap flights for the independent traveller.

www.lastminute.com
Handy site for booking a flight at short notice should you have some last-minute stags who want to join you on the weekend.

www.unmissable.com
Wide selection of activities, travel suggestions and information on festivals and racing.

www.easyjet.com
Flight-only packages at competitive prices.

www.go-fly.com
Flight-only packages at competitive prices.

SPEECHES

Centre Stage Training
www.centerstagetraining.com
Communications skills workshops run by singer and voice coach Karen Malim.

www.wantaspeech.co.uk (01472-237973)
Tailor-made speeches by scriptwriter Malcolm Perkins.

www.crispandcheerful.co.uk (0800-389 8568)
Personalized speeches and tips from speech writer
Keith Anderson.

Speeches for you (07816-230213)
Different services will help you write, prepare and
deliver your speech.

www.wordsmith.org/anagram
Make anagrams – nice ones, of course – out of the
names of principal players at the wedding.
Guarantees a few laughs.

Little Giant Encyclopaedia Of Wedding Toasts
(£6.99 Orion).

Speaking On Special Occasions
From the *Teach Yourself* series (Hodder & Stoughton).

JOKES AND QUOTATIONS

www.startingpage.com/html/quotations.html
A useful starting point with links to a bewildering
number of relevant sites.

www.famous-quotes.com
More than 300 quotations on the theme of love and
marriage alone.

www.quotationspage.com
The first ever quotation site on the web. Look under
'marriage' or 'men and women'.

www.lifeisajoke.com
Offers various categories of humour from alcohol
jokes to *The Simpsons*.

www.anyman.com
Boasts jokes with gallows humour, including some
that are darker and more cynical than the usual.

www.the-jokes.com
Subscribe to this service and have jokes sent to you.

CLOTHES

Burton (0800-731 8283)
www.burtonmenswear.co.uk
Online advice for clothes ranging from highland wear
to frock coats available in store.

Youngs (020-8327 2731)
www.youngs-hire.com
Hire suits over the internet with the help of a male
figure that you can dress in different clothes and
accessories. Also available at Suits You stores, Suits
You outlets and Suit Direct stores.

Debenhams
www.debenhams-formalhire.com
Another site that offers an interactive mannequin to
look at a variety of outfits.

Moss Bros (020-7447 7200)
www.mossbros.com
Includes a guide to formal dressing with summaries of what constitutes morning wear, black tie, etc.

Pronuptia
www.pronuptia.co.uk
Details of suits and accessories to buy and formal wear available to hire.

Austin Reed (0800-585479)
www.austinreed.co.uk
Offers a made-to-measure service, formal men's wear hire and a Visiting Personal Shopping Service.

Lords Formalwear (020-7363 1033)
www.lords-formal-wear.com
Morning, evening and highland wear to hire.

Masterhand (0800-716917)
Formal wear to hire from German occasion wear specialist.

Formal Affair
www.formalaffair.co.uk
Men's wear hire specialist, including children's wear from eighteen months.

Gary Anderson (020-7287 6661)
London-based designer specializing in formal wear, waistcoats and accessories.

Favourbrook (020-7491 2337)
www.favourbrook.com
Specialist in occasion wear, brocade and velvet jackets, and elaborate waistcoats.

Daks (020-7409 4050)
www.daks.com
Very British style from design team headed by Timothy Everest.

The Pantiles Groom (01892-548511)
www.pantilesgroom.co.uk
Winner of Best Bridal Menswear retailer award.

Anthony Formalwear (01277-651140)
www.anthonyformalwear.co.uk
Essex-based specialist offering classic and
contemporary styles.

Kilt Hire Company (0800-018 5458)
www.kilthire.com
Scottish-based company offering a full range of
highland wear and accessories.

Geoffrey Tailor (0141-331 2388)
www.geoffreykilts.co.uk
Nationwide company offering highland dress service.

Fantasy Waistcoats (0121-353 2848)
www.fantasywaistcoats.com
You name it, they can make it. The only limit is your
imagination.

Paul Smith
www.paulsmith.co.uk
The celebrities' favourite suit designer.

Giorgio Armani (020-7491 9888)
www.giorgioarmani.com
Well, it is a special occasion.

Marc Wallace (020-7731 4575)
www.marcwallace.com
Seriously smart suits in the Hurlingham collection.

Designer Direct
www.designerclothingdirect.com
Discounted designer ranges with a sales team that
will visit you at home.

Jones Bootmaker (020-7566 3070)
Don't spoil a new suit with an old pair of shoes.

GIFTS

www.connick.co.uk
Gift solutions site, including novelty cufflinks.

www.blissonline
Just key in the category and the amount you want to
spend and let Bliss do the rest.

www.hitched.com
Offers a good selection of gifts for men.

www.yourownballs.com
Does the stag weekend involve a game of golf? Order
your own personalized golf balls.

Duchamp (020-8743 5999)
Seriously nice cufflinks.

www.sfcody.com
Good for little golf gadgets for the stag weekend.

Bombay Duck (020-8749 8001)
www.bombayduck.co.uk
Gifts for him include decision dice, with heart boxes
for her.

Sonia Spencer (01367-243392)
www.soniaspencer.co.uk
Wedding accessories, including novelty cufflinks and
boxers.